AMERICAN
HUMANE

Protecting Children & Animals Since 1877

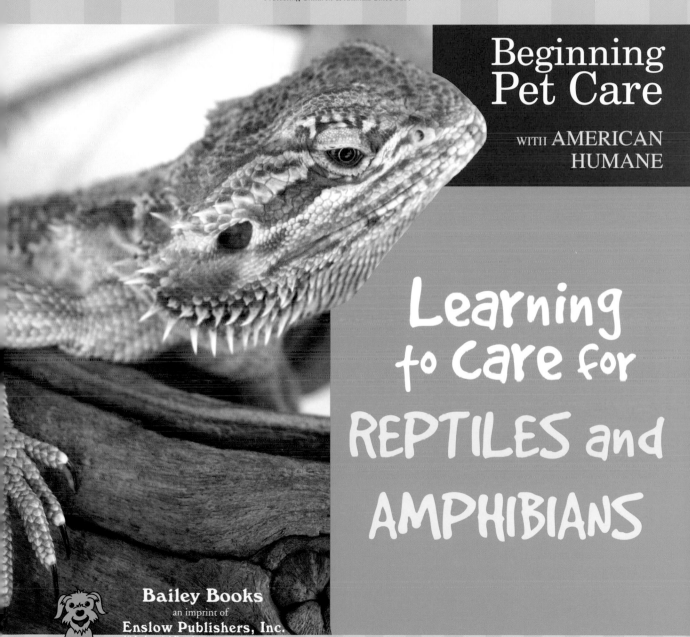

Beginning Pet Care

WITH AMERICAN HUMANE

Learning to Care for REPTILES and AMPHIBIANS

Bailey Books
an imprint of
Enslow Publishers, Inc.
40 Industrial Road
Box 398
Berkeley Heights, NJ 07922
USA
http://www.enslow.com

Felicia Lowenstein Niven

AMERICAN HUMANE

Protecting Children & Animals Since 1877

Founded in 1877, the American Humane Association is the only national organization dedicated to protecting both children and animals. Through a network of child and animal protection agencies and individuals, American Humane develops policies, legislation, curricula, and training programs — and takes action — to protect children and animals from abuse, neglect, and exploitation. To learn how you can support American Humane's vision of a nation where no child or animal will ever be a victim of abuse or neglect, visit www.americanhumane.org, phone (303) 792-9900, or write to the American Humane Association at 63 Inverness Drive East, Englewood, Colorado, 80112-5117.

To our Readers:

We have done our best to make sure all Internet Addresses in this book were active and appropriate when we went to press. However, the author and the publisher have no control over and assume no liability for the material available on those Internet sites or on other Web sites they may link to. Any comments or suggestions can be sent by e-mail to comments@enslow.com or to the address on the back cover.

Every effort has been made to locate all copyright holders of material used in this book. If any errors or omissions have occurred, corrections will be made in future editions of this book.

Bailey Books, an imprint of Enslow Publishers, Inc.

Copyright © 2011 by Enslow Publishers, Inc.

Library of Congress Cataloging-in-Publication Data

Niven, Felicia Lowenstein.
   Learning to care for reptiles and amphibians / Felicia Lowenstein Niven.
      p. cm. — (Beginning pet care with American Humane)
   Includes bibliographical references and index.
   Summary: "Readers will learn how to choose and care for reptiles and amphibians"—Provided by publisher.
   ISBN 978-0-7660-3194-4
   1. Reptiles as pets—Juvenile literature. 2. Amphibians as pets—Juvenile literature. I. Title.
   SF459.R4N58 2011
   639.3'9—dc22

                              2009026190

Printed in China

052010 Leo Paper Group, Heshan City, Guangdong, China

10 9 8 7 6 5 4 3 2 1

Illustration Credits: All animals in logo bar and boxes, Shutterstock. Bob Walters and Jeff Breeden, p. 9; Bob Walters and Laura Fields, pp. 3 (thumbnail 2), 11; Britain on View/Photolibrary, p. 12; Courtesy of Dr. Chad Hutchison/Community Animal Hospital, p. 25; © Chris Ridley/Alamy, pp. 3 (thumbnail 3), 16; © 2009 Drs. Foster and Smith, Inc.; Reprinted as a courtesy and with permission from DrsFosterSmith.com. pp. 26–27; The Image Bank/Getty Images, pp. 3 (thumbnail 5), 39; © Juniors Bildarchiv/Alamy, p. 29; Courtesy of Kristina McInerny, p. 42; Courtesy of Laura Ridgeway, pp. 3 (thumbnail 6), 34, 44; © Leszczynski, Zigmund/ Animals Animals-Earth Scenes, p. 30; © Lockwood, C.C./Animals Animals-Earth Scenes, p. 32; © maggie44/ flickr, p. 36; Mark Smith/Photo Researchers, Inc., p. 8; Mwatro/Wikimedia Commons, p. 20; Picture Partners/Photo Researchers, Inc., p. 19; Shutterstock, pp. 1, 3 (thumbnails 1, 4), 4–5, 6, 14, 18, 22, 28, 41.

Cover Illustration: Shutterstock (bearded dragon).

Table of Contents

Chapter 1
Did You Know?

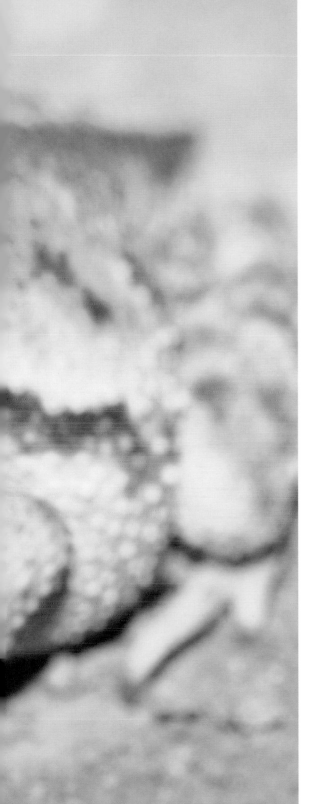

How long is a frog's tongue? If you guessed ten times as long as his body, you are right! That is true for some frogs at least. But that is nothing compared to how far frogs can jump. Some frogs can jump twenty times their body length in just one leap. That would be like you or me jumping from one end of a basketball court to another.

Do you know how to tell a frog and a toad apart? It is easy. Frogs have smooth, clammy skin. Toads have bumpy skin.

5

Did You Know?

But they have something in common. They are amphibians. The word amphibian comes from the Greek language. It means "double life." It is one way of saying that amphibians live part of their life in water and part on land.

There are more than six thousand kinds of amphibians. The largest is the Japanese giant salamander. They can grow up to five feet long.

These two poison dart frogs are colorful but dangerous!

Did You Know?

The smallest is the poison dart frog. They measure less than half an inch. Of course, you would not bring a poison dart frog or a giant salamander home. But some amphibians can be kept as pets.

So can some reptiles. There are more than eight thousand different kinds of reptiles. Reptiles can be as small as a dwarf gecko, which is less than an inch long. They can be as large as a saltwater crocodile, which weighs a ton.

Reptiles and amphibians are similar in another way. They both hatch from eggs, although some species of reptiles give birth to live young.

Reptile hatchlings look just like miniature adults. Amphibians hatch as tadpoles, which look like fish. Tadpoles live in the water and breathe through gills. As they grow into adults, tadpoles grow legs and lungs. This allows them to leave the water and live on land.

This is a dwarf or striped leaftail gecko.

Another difference between reptiles and amphibians is their skin. Reptiles have scales, and their skin is dry. Amphibians do not have scales, and their skin is moist.

Are you ready to find out more about getting a reptile or an amphibian as a pet?

Chapter 2

History of Reptiles and Amphibians

Millions of years ago, dinosaurs walked the earth. So did other reptiles and amphibians. There were turtles and crocodiles, for example. The turtles and crocodiles looked and acted a lot like they do today.

Dinosaurs, including the Tyrannosaurus Rex roamed the earth many, many years ago.

History of Reptiles and Amphibians

But the other reptiles, and amphibians, have changed a lot over hundreds of millions of years. You would not recognize them.

The first amphibians looked like fish with feet. They had lungs so that they could live on land. They also could be in water. Those creatures became the frogs and salamanders that we know today.

The first reptiles came from amphibians. At least that is what many scientists believe. Over millions of years, some amphibians became reptiles. They changed from living in the water to land. Their eggs formed thick shells to protect them. Their skin became tough, too.

For the longest time, amphibians and reptiles were wild animals. They did not live with people. But people noticed them. They used them in their stories. Snakes, for example, were sometimes good but more often evil.

10

The stegosaurus is another type of dinosaur.

The corn snake can make a great pet.

History of Reptiles and Amphibians

In ancient Egypt, frogs were good. People thought they meant life. The Egyptians would even bury frogs with the dead.

But you will find more reptiles and amphibians in many households in the United States, too. They continue to fascinate us, and they are popular pets. The best thing that you can do before you bring home any pet is to explore all of his or her needs.

Chapter 3
Getting a Reptile or Amphibian

Reptiles and amphibians can make good pets and are pretty easy to keep clean. They are quiet animals and are interesting to watch.

There are many different kinds, too. If you want a reptile, you can get a snake, lizard, turtle, or tortoise. If you want an amphibian, you can get a frog, toad, salamander, or newt.

Be gentle when you hold your pet.

Getting a Reptile or Amphibian

Snakes

There are many kinds of snakes in all different sizes. Some, like corn snakes, are safe to own. Others, like anacondas, are too dangerous to have as a pet. Check with an expert on which one to choose.

Of course, snakes are not right for everyone. For one thing, they eat other animals. If you are not ready to feed your snake a mouse, then a snake is not for you. Also, if someone in your family is scared of snakes, do not get one. It will be a problem.

Lizards

Maybe a lizard is a good choice. There are more than four thousand kinds. They range in size from just a few inches to the Komodo dragon, which can grow to ten feet long! Do not be fooled by those

If you do not want to feed your pet live crickets, then a lizard may not be the best pet for you.

cute little hatchlings. They may start out tiny but they can become big fast.

Some lizards can be handled. These include leopard geckos, bearded dragons, and green anoles. Other lizards, like chameleons or iguanas, should be left to the experts. They do not like to be handled as much. They also need a lot more care. They can even get aggressive.

16

Getting a Reptile or Amphibian

Depending on their size, lizards may eat greens or live prey. If you do not want to feed crickets to a lizard, choose another pet.

Finally, lizards can live for a long time. A leopard gecko can live for twenty years. Make sure you are ready to make that commitment.

Turtles and Tortoises

Turtles need to live near water. Tortoises live in dry areas. Both can be kept as pets, but here are some problems to consider.

First, turtles are very messy. Second, they can grow to be very big.

Third, and this is the most important, turtles carry a type of dangerous bacteria called salmonella. Salmonella are tiny creatures that live inside the turtle, where its body digests food. Turtles are not the only ones with salmonella. Lizards can also carry salmonella.

Small turtles can make good pets, but be sure to wash your hands before and after touching your pet.

Salmonella does not harm the turtle or lizard. But it makes people very sick. It can even be deadly!

The government has rules about pet turtles. You are not allowed to own a turtle that measures less than four inches. That is because young children might put a small turtle into their mouths.

You can protect yourself from salmonella by washing your hands. If you own a turtle or tortoise,

Getting a Reptile or Amphibian

wash after you touch her—each and every time. And even though you love your pet, never ever kiss her.

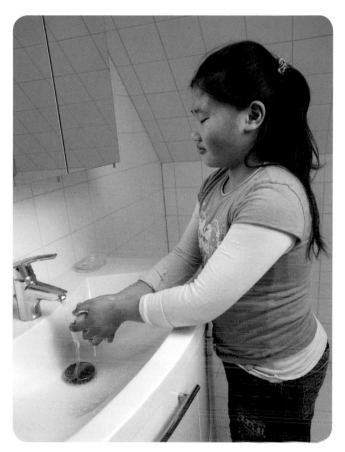

It is very important to wash your hands after touching any pet.

Since salmonella is found naturally in turtles, take that into account when choosing a pet. A turtle is not a good choice if people in your house are very young, old, or sick. Salmonella could be deadly for them.

You will need to provide a home with clean water for your turtle. But you also need water

Some frogs are better for beginner pet owners. Ask your pet store which is the best for you.

for your land tortoise. A tortoise needs to soak its entire body at least once a week. Finally, turtles and tortoises can live for fifty years. Some kinds can live for a hundred years! Make sure you are ready for this kind of commitment.

Frogs and Toads

There are many different kinds of frogs. Some are better for beginners. These include the African dwarf frog. Do not confuse that with the African clawed frog, which is illegal in some states.

Getting a Reptile or Amphibian

Frogs and toads eat insects. Big ones even eat mice. Are you ready to feed them what they need? Otherwise a frog or toad may not be the right pet.

Finally, frogs and toads can live from four to fifteen years. Make sure you can take care of your pet for this time.

Salamanders and Newts

Salamanders and newts look a little like lizards. But while lizards are reptiles, salamanders and newts are amphibians. They do not have nails on their toes. Some live in water and some on land. Others like to be in a place where there is both water and land.

If you would like to hold your pet, a salamander or newt is not for you. Just as you would not pick up a fish, you would not pick up a salamander or newt.

Salamanders and newts cannot be handled!

Getting a Reptile or Amphibian

Making the Decision

To choose the right pet, figure out what is most important. Do you want an animal that likes to be held? Do you have a large or small space? Learn all that you can about the type of animal so you know whether it is a good fit.

Also, some reptiles and amphibians are not allowed in certain states. For others, you need a permit. Check with your local Fish and Game or Wildlife Department for the rules.

Where can you get a reptile or amphibian? You can sometimes find them at an animal shelter or rescue group. These places charge a fee to cover their costs.

You can find them at breeders. Breeders are listed on the Internet.

Pet shops also sell reptiles and amphibians.

Getting a Reptile or Amphibian

Sometimes the animals at pet shops are treated well, but sometimes they are not. Wherever you go to get your pet, pay attention. Is the place clean? Ask a lot of questions. Make sure you are getting a healthy pet.

Please do not take your reptile or amphibian from the wild. And never release a pet into the wild if you cannot care for it anymore. Both are very bad for the environment.

Once you have chosen your pet, make an appointment with a veterinarian as soon as you can. You will want to find a specialist in amphibians and reptiles. Contact your local veterinary medical association for names.

On the first visit, your vet will examine your pet. He will make sure that your pet is healthy and probably discuss the pet's diet and care. Best of all, the vet can answer your questions. Write them down so you do not forget what you want to know.

Find a vet that will take care of reptiles and amphibians.
Once you do, bring your pet to the vet right away.

Chapter 4

Health and Exercise

Most reptiles and amphibians need some sort of heat lamp. All reptiles and amphibians should have a terrarium. Ask your vet which is the best kind for your pet.

Your pet is coming home! Are you ready?

You will need the right home for him. Reptiles and amphibians are cold-blooded. Their body temperature changes with how warm or cold it is around them.

Most amphibians are okay between 60 and 70 degrees Fahrenheit. Reptiles are usually comfortable between 68 and 95 degrees. But some tropical species need to be between 80 and 100 degrees.

You may need a heat lamp to warm the cage. But you do not want to burn your pet.

27

Health and Exercise

Make sure the lamp is at least eighteen inches above the cage floor or use a divider screen. Keep the lamp at one end so the animal can move closer or farther away as needed. Keep a thermometer there, too. Then you can see how hot it is.

Some turtles need an area in their terrarium where they can swim.

Health and Exercise

Light is also important. Both amphibians and reptiles need light for healthy skin. But the kind of light that comes through the glass of his cage is not enough. You probably need to shine a special lightbulb that produces ultraviolet (UV) rays. Remember to shut it off at night so your pet can sleep.

Make your pet's home as close to nature as you can. Include hiding spaces and bedding. Different pets need different types of bedding. Certain types of bedding can be harmful to some animals and not to others. Research what your pet needs.

Heat lamps are very important. Be sure to check with your vet or a worker at a pet store to see if you need a heat lamp.

Health and Exercise

You might need an area where there is just water. Amphibians need to be near or in water. But the water must be very clean. Water from the faucet is not clean or pure enough. Amphibians can absorb impurities, or pollutants, through their skin and become sick.

A charcoal filter will help clean the water. Or, you could buy purified water. You can also test your water with a kit from the pet store.

Your pet will need clean bedding and a place to hide.

Health and Exercise

Make sure your pet has enough room to move around in his new home. There should be places to climb and burrow.

Amphibians and many reptiles will get enough exercise in their homes. But it helps larger reptiles to walk around. If you let your pet out of his cage, watch him closely so he does not get hurt or lost.

It is important to keep your pet's home clean, too. Your pet will go to the bathroom in his cage. Clean that up every day. Also, remove any uneaten food, which can add bacteria. Change the water bowl every day, too. If you have an aquatic reptile or amphibian, you will need to change the water in their tank every one to two weeks.

Completely replace the bedding every week. That is also when you should disinfect the cage. Your vet can tell you the safest products to use. You can also research household products that would work best and destroy bacteria.

These boys are holding a corn snake.

Health and Exercise

Your vet can tell you what to feed your pet. Amphibians usually eat live food. This may include worms, minnows, guppies, and newborn mice or rats. Reptiles are sometimes meat eaters and other times plant eaters. Meat eaters enjoy goldfish, mealworms, crickets, mice or rats. Plant eaters like leafy greens and vegetables. Some animals need both plants and animals. Find out exactly what your pet needs.

Sometimes when you feed live food, there is not enough nutrition. There is a way to get around that. You can feed the prey nutritious cereal or vegetables just before you feed it to your pet. You can even "dust" crickets with vitamin and mineral powders. This will help your pet get the vitamins she needs.

Having a clean home and good food will help your pet stay healthy. But there are a few more things to know.

Your pet snake will need fresh water every day and a hiding place.

Reptiles shed their skin. This happens whenever they grow or it wears down. In snakes and some lizards, the entire skin comes off in a single piece. Other times, your pet will shed pieces of skin.

34

Health and Exercise

You may notice your pet rubbing against a rock or rough surface. This helps the skin to come off. You can help, too. Mist the cage to keep it damp. That will make shedding easier; so will a bowl with a couple inches of water for soaking.

Finally, you will want to spend time with your pet. With amphibians, that means watching them play. Reptiles can be held. Some like to be held more than others. Bearded dragons, box turtles, and king snakes like to be picked up. Wash your hands before and after you touch your pet—each and every time! This will keep you, and her, safe from spreading germs.

Importantly, talk to your vet and schedule yearly visits. This will help keep your pet healthy.

Chapter 5

Problems and Challenges

Owning a reptile or amphibian is fun. It is also challenging. You may face some problems. Here are some common ones.

If you think your pet is sick, take him to the vet right away!

Problems and Challenges

Parasites

Have you heard of stomach worms, roundworms, and hookworms? These are parasites that live inside reptiles and amphibians. They can make your pet sick.

The best way to prevent parasites is to keep a very clean cage. But if your pet does get them, see your vet. She can prescribe medicine. You will also need to clean the cage. Otherwise, the parasites will be back!

Skin Problems

Parasites can also affect your pet's skin. In reptiles, one common parasite is the mite.

If you look hard, you can see the mites. Put your pet on a piece of white paper. Then, gently rub he or she. You might see the mites fall off.

Problems and Challenges

You also might see them in your pet's water. Sometimes reptiles soak in water to try to drown the mites.

If your reptile has mites, you need to clean the cage very well. Your vet can help you with treatment for your pet.

Fungal Infection

Do you have an amphibian with open sores? Maybe you notice white or yellow furry growths? This could be a fungal infection.

If this happens, take your pet to the vet. She will give you the right treatment. It might be a special bath. You will also want to clean the tank very well.

Health problems are one type of challenge you may face. Sometimes you might also have problems with behavior.

Problems and Challenges

Skittish Pets

Most reptiles are skittish when you first get them. They are not used to being held. They may not feel safe. They may squirm and try to jump. They may even poop on you.

Be careful and always hold them over a table. Do not drop your pet. Put him down gently. Just spend a little time each day holding him until he gets used to you.

Scratching and Biting

Scratches can happen when your pet's claws are too long. While rocks

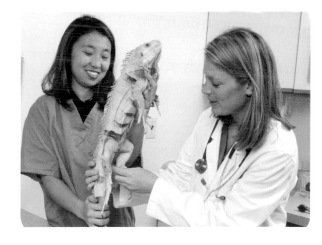

Your vet will be able to answer any questions you may have about your pet.

are great claw trimmers, they do not always do the job! You can keep your pet's claws trimmed by clipping off just the tip. This may be a job for the vet.

Bites can happen for a lot of reasons. Your pet may be scared or stressed. He may be in breeding season. He may even react to a color you are wearing.

Pet snakes may bite because they are hungry. Your hand might smell like food.

If your pet bites you, wash the area right away. Then apply an antibiotic ointment. If the bite becomes red or swells, you could have an infection. To be safe, contact your family doctor if your pet bites you and breaks the skin.

More Than one Pet

Many amphibians and reptiles like to be alone. But if you decide to put two or more together, there

Problems and Challenges

are some things you should know.

Males sometimes fight with each other. Even animals of the same species might not get along. Do not put more than one male in

Ask an adult to help you with your pet.

any group. Also, watch your pets closely. You might have to move them to separate cages.

Finally, make sure that the cage or area is not overcrowded. There should be hiding places for each pet. Make sure there is room to move around. Include items to climb on and places to bask near the light.

Chapter 6
A Lifelong Responsibility

Sami and her gecko,
St. Rose.

A Lifelong Responsibility

When ten-year-old Sami plays hide and seek with her friends, there is "someone" watching. It is her eighteen-month-old leopard gecko, St. Rose.

"If you watch the lizard closely, you can tell where they are hiding," said Sami's mom Kristina. "She will stare at the kids."

Sami will tell you plenty of other interesting facts about St. Rose. "Her tail stores fat. She can go for days without eating. We feed her crickets and sometimes mealworms. St. Rose is a hunter. When there's a cricket in her cage, she stays really still. Then she pounces!"

David, age twelve, also enjoys feeding his pet corn snake, Kellogg.

"It's really interesting," he said. "Snakes do not have teeth. Kellogg actually unhinges her jaw. Then her neck wiggles her prey down through her body. After she eats, we don't hold her for a few days so we don't disturb her."

A Lifelong Responsibility

Kellogg has grown two feet in the two years that David has owned her. "She should grow to about four feet and live up to fourteen years," he said.

David has made a lifelong commitment to Kellogg, as Sami has to St. Rose. You, too, can bring reptiles or amphibians into your life and your family. Make them a good safe and clean home, and they will entertain you for years to come.

David and his corn snake, Kellogg.

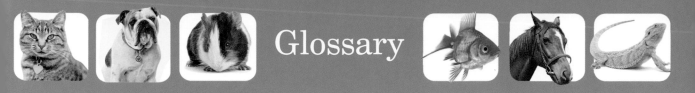

amphibian—A cold-blooded animal that starts life in the water breathing through gills and in time breathes through lungs on land.

bacteria—A very tiny living thing that causes disease.

burrow—To dig a hole to hide.

cold-blooded—Having a body temperature that changes with the temperature of the surroundings.

disinfect—To clean so there is no bacteria.

parasites—Living things that feed off of another animal.

prey—An animal that is eaten by another animal.

reptile—A type of cold-blooded animal with scales or horny plates that breathes via lungs and lays eggs.

skittish—Nervous and restless.

species—A specific kind of animal.

Further Reading

Books

Clarke, Barry, and Laura Buller. *Amphibian*. New York: DK Children, 2005.

Gruber, Beth. *Reptile Style*. Mankato, Minn.: Compass Point Books, 2004.

Randolph, Joanne. *Snakes*. New York: Rosen Publishing Group, 2007.

Further Reading

Internet Addresses

American Humane Association
<http://www.americanhumane.org>

National Geographic: Amphibians
<http://animals.nationalgeographic
.com/animals/amphibians.html>

National Geographic: Reptiles
<http://animals.nationalgeographic
.com/animals/reptiles.html>